Big George

Big George

THE AUTOBIOGRAPHY OF AN ANGEL

Hay House, Inc.
Carlsbad, CA

Published and distributed in the United States by:

Hay House, Inc.
P.O. Box 5100
Carlsbad, CA 92018-5100
(800) 654-5126 • (800) 650-5115 (fax)

Book design by: Highpoint Graphics, Inc., Claremont, CA

Library of Congress Cataloging-in-Publication Data

Jennings, James.
    Big George : the autobiography of an angel.
      p. cm.
    ISBN 1-56170-121-1 (hardcover) • ISBN 1-56170-617-5 (tradepaper)
    1. Infants (Newborn)--Fiction. 2. Angels--Fiction. 3. Death--Fiction
    I. Title. II. Title: Autobiography of an angel.
PS3552.I39B54 1994   94-33993
813'.54--dc20   CIP

ISBN 1-56170-617-5

02 01 00 99   12 11 10 9
First Printing, November 1994
9th Printing, August 1999

Printed in the United States of America

"We can do no great things,
only small things with great love."

—MOTHER TERESA

"Love one another..."

— BIG GEORGE

Before I formed you in the womb,
I knew you; before you were born,
I set you apart.

Baby Heaven

"To become a full-fledged angel," our Father said to me and a group of baby angels in Heaven's nursery, which is apart from Heaven proper, "you must first serve an apprenticeship. This is why some of you will be leaving to be born of the flesh of earthly mothers and fathers. That which you are, which is Spirit, will reveal itself in human form. You will be angels disguised as humans."

A baby spirit—who was not an angel, but who was my friend—said to me with greater happiness, "I'm listening to my parents. They are in the process of conceiving me. Pat's my mom's name. She said that if I'm a girl, I'll be named Heather Marie. Dad says if I'm a boy he wants to call me Jalil Damon. Dad says it means 'great friend.'"

And *pop!* The baby spirit was gone before I had a chance to tell it I liked both names. No matter. Perhaps we'll meet again on Earth. If not, we will when we return home to Heaven.

Our bodies have not been conceived yet. Father tells us baby angels with a chuckle that we're just gleams in our human fathers' eyes, whatever that means. Soon, Father says.

A guardian angel tending Baby Heaven said I'd be an accident. I was asking the angel what an accident was when Father hushed the angel, saying to me that some angels talk too much.

I am excited, of course, about my apprenticeship being served on Earth, though I'll miss Heaven. That word was explained to me by a guardian angel. An emotion. The angel said he had served his apprenticeship on Earth, and he told me that as a human I'd know many emotions. But he said not to worry about it. "You will be as a human but seven paths of the Earth's moon; however, the moments of your human life shall be precious and touch the lives of many—"

And Father was then beside the angel, admonishing, "I alone count the days of man, My child." And the angel blushed like a yellow-red dimming sun and departed.

Father then said to me, "Human life, My little angel, is not measured by the moon's path, but by the strength of human love and divine intercession." I knew of love—Father is Love. Strength? Father's smile imparted its meaning to me. I asked Father about those moon paths, but He smiled it off by calling the angel's words loose talk. "I've problems here, too, My child," He said. "Human life creates habits in My children—angels and spirits alike—that are often difficult to shed."

"Will I return from my apprenticeship, Father, with these habits You speak of?"

Father touched me and I glowed goldenly. "No, My child. I have given man many powers, and he has of late been prone to find false promise in the powers of his mind. He has strayed from the power of his heart. I have chosen you to impart a reminder to man that the greatest power lies not in his mind but in his heart."

Me! A special angel. "I will do Your bidding, Father."

"The moment is nigh, child." Then Father gave me some last-moment instructions.

The *pop!* tickled. So this is what dark is like. Snug. Mother feels good. Gee, I like being human.

昭 昭 昭

For you created my inmost being;
you knit me together in my mother's womb.

Six Months Later

DAY 1

What an experience that was!
I hear voices more clearly now.
Am I born?

"You have a beautiful boy, Sharon."

"Is he okay, doctor?" A little different in the way
she sounds, but definitely Mother.

I'm a boy? Mmm. Guess I'm born as a human.

"He's tiny, Sharon. We'll have to get him cleaned up, and then warm him up in an incubator. Don't you worry, we'll do all we can for him. Hazel, suction and weigh him, please."

It's all so strange. Not what I was told to expect. *Something's wrong.* Father said that human babies cry when born. Why am I not crying? Is it because I'm an angel, and angels don't cry? I wish I were still inside Mother. They're saying a lot of things I don't understand.

"Six hundred eighty-two grams, doctor. Pound and a half!" The voice of a female.

"We're going to place him in an incubator, Sharon." It's the first voice I heard clearly. "Just have to see how things go."

"Can I touch him, doctor?" Mother.

"Sure you can, Sharon, for a moment. Have you named him?" The man Mother calls doctor.

"His name is George."

I feel Mother. But it is a different feel. *You will know your mother's touch, Father said. You are the flesh of your mother, your father, on Earth. You are the Spirit of Me, your heavenly Father.* I feel better now that Mother has touched me.

Mother's touch leaves me, and I feel movement almost like when Mother would walk with me inside her, except now I am being moved in a different way.

"Any chance for him, doctor?" A woman's voice.

"Always a chance, Maggie. Heart seems strong. Let's get him on a respirator and see how well he's breathing. Then I'm going to phone regional neonatal to come pick him up...that is, if he lasts that long."

"George, huh?" The Maggie voice. "Well, little fellow, why don't we just call you Big George. That okay with you?"

I'm not real sure what *big* is, but it sounds okay to me. I wish Father were here; I'm unsure of myself.

"I am here, George."

Father! What are they doing to me? Is all this necessary to being human? I thought babies just came into being and lived warmly in their mother's love, and gooed and gaahed and slept a lot and drank warm milk. They have taken me away from Moth—

"Slow down, George. Remember that you are My messenger; you are more angel than human."

Well, Father, now that I know how it is, if You'd given me a choice, I'd have picked one or the other. Now what are they doing to me?

"One thing at a time, George. First, you are human enough to have a choice. Even as an angel, you have a choice. Remember Lucifer? He had a choice, and he chose evil. Sometimes I'd like to say, 'Do it My way or not at all,' but I have never been rudely authoritative, child, and I don't intend to begin now. Second, you're in an incubator. It is, for an easy explanation, an area somewhat like your mother's womb. It'll keep you warm and help your human body to breathe. You were born three months—Earth time—too soon, and you need its help."

Born too soon, Father!

"Yes, child. I was in a hurry to get My message delivered. Now, I must go. Do My bidding. In an emergency, George, you may speak to Me through prayer, as do all My human children who love Me. Oh...I like your human name. Fits you."

Fits me, Father?

"Yes," Father said. "Big George." He winked and left me, without telling me what an *emergency* was.

"Bill, this is Jack in Tupelo. I've got an emergency for you. We're going to need life-support transfer to regional. He's a tiny one, a pound and a half, rather healthy except for his heart. Patient's name is Hawkins, newborn of Sharon Hawkins...Hey, that's great. Angel Two's in the area, huh? Well, we're ready to transfer when Angel Two gets here. See you, Bill."

That was the voice of the doctor here. Sharon Hawkins is my mother's name. Well, now I know what an emergency is—*I* am! They have angels? He said one is in the area.

"Let's get an umbilical IV going, Charlie."

Not snug in here like Mother, but better than where I was. I am sleepy—

Owwh! What in Heaven was that? My tummy! So much going on here that Father never told us baby angels about. Well, I'm a messenger, so perhaps things are different for special angels. I can see now that it's going to be double work being an angel and a human down here. I'm tempted to complain, but angels shouldn't complain...I don't think. Tempted. Father explained that emotion, saying that as humans we would be continually tempted to do things we shouldn't do.

"There, little fellow, that should help your heart calm down. You get some sleep now."

* * *

I must have slept. Heavens! What is that sound? I've never heard a sound like it before. Sounds like the screaming of a shooting star. Where am I?

"Regional base, this is Angel Two. We have a life-support infant."

"Can you give us an ETA?" Very strange voice!

"About ten to twelve minutes out."

"We'll have rear loading zone two cleared for you, Angel Two."

"That's a roger, regional. How's he doing back there, doctor?"

"He's hanging in there. But don't ask me how. I[ ] a miracle this tiny guy ever took his first breath. H[ ] be lucky to make the day."

Well, doctor, if it takes the day for me to deliver Father's message—or two days or whatever—you ca[ ] sure I'll hang in there, as you say.

That angel sure has a strange name. Angel [ ] And I thought I knew everyone in Heaven. Whe[ ] my mother? *Would someone please tell me what is g[ ]*

Maybe if I do some kicking like I did inside Mother I can get some attention.

"That's it, little fellow. Raise the dickens. That siren noise bothering you?" So that's the screaming. That? Siren? Makes a little sense to me, but not much. "Bet you miss your mother already." *You'd better believe I do!* "Well, I imagine she and your daddy will be coming to be with you soon."

It's a good thing I've been studying English the past six months, or I wouldn't know a word they're saying. Heaven's language is better. We all spoke the same way there, knew all the same words, and our words were Heaven's music.

A lot of unknown people around me. I miss Mother. I'm happy now that that emotion was explained to me in Heaven, or I wouldn't know what I was feeling. Now what? My tummy just did flip-flop.

"Let's put him here next to Jalil."

Jalil! So my friend made it here as a boy. If Jalil is

here, things must be all right. I wonder if he came down too soon? He left Baby Heaven before I did, I know, but how long before me I don't remember. Time isn't important in Heaven. If it wasn't for Father keeping track of His human children, in Heaven we'd probably never hear of time. Ha! I talk as though I'm still in Heaven.

Hi, Jalil. No response. He must be asleep, as I'm sure he can still understand Heaven's language. I'll try him again later.

I'm not comfortable. I don't think this body fits me. Too small, as humans say. Mother used to complain while I was inside her that her clothes no longer fit, that they were too small and it made her uncomfortable. That's the way my chest feels, like it's too small for my heart. *Ouch! Hey, stop that! Ouch! Hey, don't you understand plain thought? I said to stop that! That doesn't—ouch!—feel good.* There's that feeling again...I want to do something, but can't.

"Sorry, sweetheart," a beautiful voice says. "That's the only time you'll feel Susan sticking you. We make sure that none of our little ones feel any pain while they're here."

Whew! I'm glad to hear that. I'm learning more of their Earth-only words, and *pain's* one of them I don't like.

"I love the way you talk to them, Susan."

"As I told you before, Dr. Miles, babies like being talked to."

There is a golden sparkle to her voice. I like this one. Well, she can tell Doctor for me that I'm human, and all humans, Father said, like being talked to.

I feel Susan move away from me. "Jalil, you have a new friend here beside you," she says. "His name is George, but I was told that another nurse, one where he was born, tagged him with the name 'Big George.'" A nurse must be something like a guardian angel, Earth-style. "Poor darling, Dr. Miles told me your parents are on their way to be with you."

I think I'll ask her about my parents. *What about mine, Susan?*

Susan laughs.

"Really, Susan, this place could use cheering up, but spontaneous giggling?" Dr. Miles' voice again. He laughs, too.

"Sorry, Dr. Miles, but when I was talking to Jalil—" She laughs again. "Well, I would've sworn Big George said, 'What about mine, Susan?' You know, like he was asking about his parents. Okay, I'm nuts. Too many hours, too many babies." She laughs again.

How about that? I was beginning to wonder if anyone on Earth could understand angel language. Well, Father did say that humans with pure love in their hearts could hear His angels.

ℱℱℱ

DAY 2

*J*alil's parents are here. Mine aren't. I'm lying here listening to them talk to a doctor and Susan.

"Jim...Pat. I'm Dr. Miles, chief pediatrician for neonatal. I see you've met Susan."

"Yes. Glad to meet you, doctor. Yes, Susan showed us around, how to scrub, where the gowns are, told us a few things about the center. I never realized so many babies were here."

"We average a few over fifty. They come from four states. I'm told that you and Pat are from Dallas."

"Yes. As someone may have told you, our son was born in Jackson, Tennessee, and then was moved here the next morning. Well, of course you'd know that. We were traveling to Georgia. I'm a writer and speaker. The job keeps me on the road a lot. What kind of outlook do you have for our son?"

"He's a very sick infant, as you were told. Frankly, Jim, although we've run a lot of cultures since yesterday, we're not sure what we're dealing with. I suspect an adult strain of pneumonia. There could be problems."

"What kind of problems, doctor?" A woman. Pat?

"Well, Pat, it's not good. Pneumonia in itself is bad enough, but we're almost helpless to treat an infant for an adult strain. The usual antibiotics are toxic to infants. Now, I'm not saying we can't treat him, just that it may pose problems."

I like Pat's voice. Sweet.

"Are you saying, doctor, that he may not survive?"

That's Jim asking.

"We never say an infant won't survive. Thank God, I learned early on here that miracles take place almost daily. I'm just saying your child's chances—medically—are too slim to quote a percentage. Right now, we may be looking at a few hours, a few days. I don't know. He may even survive. Now, I'm not trying to upset you or to give you false hope, but previous experience in identical cases...well, I'm sorry, have all proved terminal. Your son's lungs are filled with fluid, and the infection has apparently advanced rapidly; it could have damaged other vital organs. I just can't say yet. Again, I'm sorry. Wish I could be more optimistic for you."

"May we stay with him, doctor?"

"Of course, Pat. Well, I've some rounds to make. I'll be talking with you again."

Silence...

"Jim, Pat." Susan's voice. "He's a good doctor. One of the best. Don't think for a moment that he's given up on your son. He'll move medical mountains to find some way to treat the virus. He's saved others—seemingly hopeless cases—with inventive medicine. He's a brilliant man. But he has this thing about preparing parents for the worst. There's not a doctor alive who doesn't lose patients, but...well, few doctors are faced with the number of critically ill patients that Dr. Miles is. It's not an easy job."

"I can understand that," Jim says. "Hey, would you look at Jalil. He sure doesn't look sick."

I feel Susan smile. Funny. My senses are much as they were in Heaven, and Father had told us that as humans we'd lose some of our heavenly senses. Perhaps the reason I still have heavenly senses is because I'm an angel in a human body.

"Well, in bed one we have our smallest patient. We call him Big George. He weighs a pound and a half. Your son's in bed two, and he's our biggest patient at eight-and-a-half pounds. It seems appropriate that they're near each other. Neither looks sick. Both beautiful boys."

Beep! Beep! Beep! Beep! Beep! Beep!

There's that *beep!* again. I've heard it a lot of the time I've been here. Several times it was right above me, and—Heavens!—my little 'me' hurt! The *beep!* is someplace else, but not far from me.

"Life-support failure alarm," Susan says. "You'll hear it a lot while you're here. Don't allow it to upset you. Babies get a little stubborn about breathing sometimes. When they do, their alarms go off. But right now I'd better hurry and help them out...Oh, I'm sorry, Jim, but you and Pat'll need to wait in the small waiting room or outside whenever the alarm goes off. I'll come get you when the crisis is over. But if you go outside, be sure to scrub and change gowns before coming back in."

Silence again.

I hear faint voices not far away, but I can't make them out.

Jalil, are you awake?

No answer again. Surely he can hear me. He could in heaven...why not here?

Father, are You there?

"Father's busy. What is it, George?"

Gabriel! What are you doing here?

"Father sent me. You are concerned for Jalil. Where is your faith, child? Have you found comfort as a human and forgotten Father's instructions?"

No, Gabriel. It's pretty difficult finding comfort as a human. Half of me's comfortable, and the other half is unsure.

"What does Father say of unsureness?"

When in doubt, trust.

"And you were sent here for...?"

To deliver a message that love is the most powerful force on Earth and in the heavens.

"Well, George, millions of humans are calling on Father, each with either some real or imagined problem. You being an angel, don't you think you could ring Father's bell less often? Now, I must go, and you must do Father's bidding. As Father said, stay in contact with Him by prayer...but just make sure your prayers are mostly in praise of Him. Other prayers should be in an emergency only. After all, George, you are an angel and do not have the insecurity of humans. You know what we say in Heaven..."

I know...no matter.

Gabriel's smile makes the lights seem dim. "Yes, my brother. No matter. Nothing matters but our Father."

Gabriel went into the light. Countless angels in Heaven, and Father sends pearly Gabriel to see me. I call for help and I get a lecture. But Gabriel loves me, loves Father. He is a good angel.

Jim and Pat are back. Wish they would say hello to me.

"Is the baby okay, Susan?" Pat asks.

I feel Susan's sadness. "No, I'm sorry, but she went back to Heaven."

Why is Susan sad? There is nothing wrong with going back to Heaven. Gee, Earth is a strange place.

I don't think I'll ever understand the way humans react to things.

Jim and Pat were beside Jalil each time I woke up the rest of the day. Mom and Dad still aren't here.

৪৯ ৪৯ ৪৯

Praise the Lord, you his angels,
you mighty ones who do his bidding,
who obey his word.

DAY 3

ather said that Earth had light and darkness, but for the Earth days I've been here, it has constantly been as bright as Heaven. Well, almost. It wouldn't be so bad if humans didn't have to sleep, which was no problem in Baby Heaven, but in this bright place, as a human, I'm having trouble sleeping a lot. I slept well inside Mother. Not sleeping well, I've been doing a lot of listening, and what I just heard disturbs me.

Susan was telling Pat and Jim that some people don't like for the staff to say "Went back to Heaven," that it's written in Father's Book that only the Son of Man has ever seen Father and Heaven. Well, the angels—and I'm one—have surely seen Heaven, and as humans are of Father, the spirit has seen Heaven. Man loses knowledge of Heaven, Father said, because he is susceptible to sin from the moment he is born. I'm exempt, of course, unless I should fall from Father's grace as Lucifer did. Now, I'm not that smart as a human, but I believe that Father's Son, who is a part of Father, was telling us that only he who is without sin, who is in the grace of love, like Jesus, can know or have memory of Father and Heaven. Too, I do know that Father often remarked to us baby angels, "Each of you is as My Son." I knew then and I know now—though why I don't know—that Father sees in us—humans and spirits alike—the image of His Son.

You are curious, aren't you? Okay. As I have seen Father, what does He look like? Well, I heard Him describe Himself one day. I mean, to me He just looked like Himself. He said He looked like man.

"But, Father," quizzed another baby angel, "man has different faces—how can You look like all men?" Silly little angel! Just goes to prove that angels don't know everything like Father does. I could have answered that one—Father is able to do anything He wants to do!

Father, however, was patient. "My face is the face of Love, and when man's heart is filled with love, the face he wears will be My face." Was Father saying that each of us sees Him conceptually, that Father is the mirrored image of man's heart when man loves? I think so, and I want to obey Father so that I may always look into the face of Love.

Sin? Father said that sin was *bad*, that bad was anything against our nature, and our nature is the nature of Father, who created us. I believe, too, young as I am, that I have been tempted to sin. Father told me that I would be. Every time one of these big people stick my body with those things they call needles and make me hurt, I am tempted to stick them back and see how they like hurting, but I know

I shouldn't, so that must be the sin Father was talking about. Rule number One for me, if I want to keep on seeing Father, is not to want to stick people. Yet, they are sticking me! I can see why we humans, even half-humans, as I am, are tempted to sin against Father.

Here comes Jim. He is looking down at me. Father? Jim looks like Father! I mean, I see Jim as Father explained: *When the heart is filled with love, the face he wears will be My face.*

Please touch me, Jim. I don't know for truth why, but I need another human's touch. Perhaps it's because inside Mother I came to be secure in human touching.

He is! He is! He's nudging my finger! Got him!

"Pat, Big George has taken hold of my finger, and he's holding it. Gosh, look at his tiny fingers! Tiny, but perfectly formed."

Jim, if I could talk as humans, I'd tell you that I'm just like you, only smaller. Father said that babies can be compared to Earth, that Earth is tiny in the Heavens but dearest to Father.

"He is precious," Pat says. "Where are his parents? I haven't seen them here."

Susan says, "They live in Mississippi, about one hundred miles from here. Dr. Miles says they are poor."

Poor? Oh good! My parents shall inherit the Earth. I wonder if Jim and Pat are poor.

"Is he going to make it?" Jim asks, apparently of Susan.

I can't see Susan, but I can feel the love in her voice. "There's always hope. It's what this center is all about. We have the best medical technology there is, but hope—faith in God—is the real miracle here. We can keep Big George and others like him alive with life-support systems, help them sometimes with medication, but the miracle of those who graduate is hope. I—I'm sorry. I don't mean to sound like I'm preaching."

I understand hope. Father told me that hope is the assigning of faith to trouble.

What Jim said puzzles me. *Is he going to make it?* Make it—where to? Am I not here? Of course I am. Make it back to Heaven? Nothing shall keep me from doing the will of Father. My Father said, "Child, as your apprenticeship, I bade you to go to Earth, where you will serve as the spirit of a newborn human baby. As this human child, you will face great adversity. Through love, you will overcome your trial." The will of Father. Nothing else matters. All are of the Father; only the flesh of man is of the Earth.

"Jim, honey, being as Big George's parents are poor and don't have the money to stay here, couldn't we do something to help them financially?"

Money? Father had told me that humans place a lot of emphasis on money. So that explains it. You don't have money, you're poor. But Father said that having a lot of money isn't necessarily being rich. Still a little puzzling to me, but at least I know now that poor has something to do with money.

"I don't see why not," Jim answers. "I'll see if we can offer them help...that is, once they get here. I'll try to do it without offending them."

As I don't understand all of what they're talking about, perhaps I shouldn't relate it, but I feel there is some importance to it, or they wouldn't talk this much about it. As Father said, we'll live and learn.

"I have to get back to work," Susan says.

"I'll check on Jalil," says Pat.

"I'm going to stay with Big George for a while," says Jim. Good.

Ah! Clinging to Jim's finger is like clinging to hope!

♪ ♪ ♪

For whoever finds me finds life
and receives favors from the Lord.

DAY 4

"There's our baby, George."

I'd recognize that voice anywhere—
Mother! George? Dad? Dad has my name. Well, I
don't mind.

"Sure is tiny, ain't he, Sharon?" I like Dad's voice.
Slow and strong. "Look at that shiny black hair, curls
and all. Sure is cute."

"Mr. Hawkins. Mrs. Hawkins. My name is Susan.
I'm your son's nurse."

"Our baby gonna be all right, Miss Susan?"

"We're doing everything we can for him. He's
very brave. A real fighter."

What is *brave?* What is *fighter?* Humans use funny words. Ahhhh. Mother is touching me. Not like the feel of her when I was inside her, but the same warmth, the same heavenly feeling.

"We love him and want him, Miss Susan. He's just got to be all right."

Mmm. I must be rich, now that I understand this rich and poor talk. Father said that being loved and wanted is the greatest of riches. *I'm all right, Mother.*

"Now, Sharon, you told me you weren't gonna cry."

"I'm...I'm sorry, George. I'm trying not to."

"Mr. Hawkins?" Jim's voice.

"Yes, sir?"

"Our baby came in the same morning your son did. You sure have a beautiful boy."

"Thank you, sir. Your little baby born too soon, too?"

"Well, not at six months like Big George. Jalil was a month early. Big trouble was that after my wife's water broke, Jalil wasn't born until eight hours later.

He contracted an adult strain of pneumonia, and they haven't figured out a way to treat him yet. Drugs they use to treat adults are toxic to babies. By the way, my name's Jim. My wife is Pat. She'll be back soon. She went to check on our girls at the motel. We're not from here either. Our home's in Dallas, Texas. Jalil was born in Jackson, Tennessee, while we were traveling, and he was moved here to the center."

"I'm pleased to meet you, Jim. This's my wife, Sharon."

"Nice to meet you, Sharon. Don't you worry about the crying. We all do a lot of crying here. Well, I'll leave you alone with Big George. Anything we can do to help, you let us know. Okay?"

"Yessir. Nice of you, sir.

I'm learning more by listening. *Hey, Dad, how about a finger to hold?*

"All right if I touch him, Susan?"

"Sure it is, Mr. Hawkins. I think Big George would like that. He responds well to touching. Oh,

I hope you don't mind us calling him Big George. He's the smallest baby here now."

Dad laughs. "I kinda like the name, Susan."

Hey Dad! I can't hold your finger with my toes. That tickles.

* * *

I must have slept for a while. Good sleeping— Mother touching me. And Dad. Never felt so good in my human life. Chest doesn't hurt as much. For the last three days it'd felt like a moon had been set on my chest. That's where my heart is—my chest. Father had said that humans have a lot of pain in their hearts, but I think He understated it in my case! Come to think of it, perhaps it's because I have a big heart. Having a big heart is good, Father said. He said that humans with big hearts are dearest to Him. But I'd better stop being so pleased with myself, as Father also said having a big head can play tricks on you, make you believe you're something you're not. I just said that because every time I feel good about myself, it feels like my head is too big.

Wonder where everybody is? I can't feel Mother, and I hear no voices but Susan's, and her voice is away from me. Is Mother gone? I hope not. I need Mother. Mother is more love strength to me.

Uh-oh! The light. Well, it just blinked. It's tempting me, offering me a way out of my pain. But Father said I must remain until the message is received.

"Just got one beep from Big George." It's Susan. "That's all I need right now—lose him while his parents are here." Lose me? I don't understand. "One for the day is enough."

"Where are the parents? Anybody check on them?" I've heard this voice before, but I can't attach a name to it. Parents? Whose?

"They're in the small waiting room. I looked in on them," says Susan. "The father is just sitting there with his hands clasped, staring at the floor. The mother has the child's body, rocking it, singing to it. They've been there an hour now. Nine months. That little boy was here nine months. I can't ever begin to comprehend what a shock it is to them for him to go back to Heaven after such a struggle to live."

Susan is crying.

"Susan, why don't you take a break. Get some coffee. I'll watch your station."

"No...no, I'll be all right. I'm sorry; give me a Kleenex, will you, before one of the doctors comes in."

You need not be sorry, Susan. Father has heard your cry.

"Susan." It's Roger's father. I remembered him after hearing who the child was who went back to Heaven. "You may take our child's body now." There is much strength of love in his voice. He *knows*. I can tell by his voice. Thank you, Father. "Roger is with God now. My wife and I just needed the time to praise the Lord for His love, for allowing us to love

Roger all these months. God bless all of you for your love and dedication."

There is silence...I hear the door open and close. I feel the Son very near.

Susan says, "I really think I'm going to cry now."

The nameless voice says, "Me, too. Girl, we had that one figured lopsided. We're in here crying and grieving, and they're out there praising God."

Father is merciful to those who seek His mercy, Susan and whoever you are. Now will you two stop crying and get my parents back in here...and Jim and Pat, too.

"I'm going down after Big George's and Jalil's parents," says Susan.

Sometimes I think Susan *really* hears me. I mean, not just as an angel, but as a human.

The remainder of the day was spent in love and hope.

৪৯ ৪৯ ৪৯

Be imitations of God; therefore,
as dearly beloved children, and
live a life of love...

DAY 5

When Mother and Dad left yesterday,
they said it would be a week before they
returned. I understand a week. Inside Mother I
learned many things about Earth time. Dr. Miles told
Dad and Jim to phone anytime, and he gave them a
special phone number to use. I understand phones,
too. Mother used the phone often when I was inside
her. But Jim refused Dr. Miles' offer to use the phone,
though. I didn't clearly understand it. I'll tell you
what was said, and maybe you can understand it.

Dr. Miles had said to Jim, "Why don't you and Pat go on home and tend to your other children. We have a toll-free number you can use to phone in and check on Jalil. I know it's got to be a real hardship on your family, you all staying here."

"Thanks, doctor," Jim said, "but if it's all the same to you, we'll stay. Pat and I discussed it with our girls, and we all agreed to remain with Jalil."

"Well," Dr. Miles said, "I just wanted to offer. Most parents can't afford to stay."

Jim laughed softly.

"You can put us in that category, too. We can't really afford it, but neither can we afford not to. It's not the money for the motel and all, not really the money I'm losing from work, but more what it'll probably do to me professionally. I've begun canceling lectures, and I'm not finding much sympathy for us. In my business, canceling an obligation is tantamount to suicide. The sponsors want you there—dead or alive."

"I'm sorry to hear that, Jim," Dr. Miles said. "From experience here, I can realize your situation. Some people believe a human being, such as an infant, must have a fully developed personality in order to be dearly loved. Perhaps this kind should come here for a visit. I could show them fifty-three individuals in these beds, and no two of these children act the same. Some cry more, some less, some not at all. Some fight to live, while others just give up. They each have their quirks, their positions for sleep, other mannerisms. I'm sure you've noticed these things. Anyway, if it gets too tough, here's the 800 number."

Now, I get a little puffed up in spirit over those humans who think I haven't got a personality. Why, a guardian angel once told Father that I had a sense of humor, was stubborn when I felt the urge to be, and that I was curious for a cherub. These must be some of the humans who Father said needed an extra amount of His message.

"Show them through love, child, how to imitate Me and live a life of love."

Father wants us to be like Him. As you know, He made us in His image. He said that He wants His children on Earth to be Heaven Happy. This, He explained was for a human to think of the happiest day he has lived in joy, then double the feeling—that's Heaven happy. "Nothing," Father said, "brings greater happiness than love. Love is the Spirit's blood."

There's been a lot of *beeping* today. I beeped a few times, and so did Jalil. Neither of us, however, beeped enough to alarm the staff. It alarms Pat and Jim, though. Even one *beep!* makes them utter, "Oh no!"

I believe some of my brothers and sisters went back to Father today, but I sleep so much it's difficult to keep count of those who return. I've finally realized that I can't talk to my brothers and sisters. Being born as a human has something to do with no longer understanding angel language. Some of what I say is picked up by big humans, but not the little ones. This makes it difficult for me to keep track of who's here and who's not.

Jim and Pat have come to me several times today, and their love is powerful. Feeling the power of their love gives me hope for my message from Father. Is Jim to help me deliver it? Maybe Pat and Jalil, too?

In His last-moment instructions, Father had told me that even though I was an angel I'd have to do most of the delivering as a human. I'd asked Him why I couldn't just appear as an angel and get it done fast, and Father had laughed and told me, "Child, you have a lot to learn about man. Some men's first reaction to an angel would be to use violence to defend against the angel. Others would try to explain you away as a swamp gas—I'll explain that to you later—or as their imagination. Too, as I often say, if I sent an angel into the midst of them, where many are gathered to verify the other, their faith would die. I depend on their faith in Me to avoid mass misbehavior. Man fears the unknown, and fearing Me as being so-called unknown, well, this keeps man under My thumb. But just let Me make Myself material beside him, and man would use Me like he uses others who love. He might even try to slay Me, though this would be impossible to fulfill. Lucifer would definitely take advantage of the situation, by rushing into the hearts of men and calling My man-form a charlatan. Knowing Lucifer as I do, he'd have Me crucified if he felt he could talk some nuts into it. No, child, you must deliver the message as a human. I'll leave you aware that you are an angel in disguise, but I do not want those around you *too* aware of who you are."

"Will I still have angel power, Father?" I had asked.

"Yes, child, but only to the extent not limited by your human body. But hold up now...I don't want to hear any stories coming from Earth about you playing cherubs' games and making things fly through the air or the lights flickering on and off. You be a good angel on Earth."

Thinking about it now...you know something strange? I'm not real sure—at least the human side of me isn't—what good and bad is. Guess that's why Father says that parents are responsible for teaching their children good and bad. Of course, I know that bad is sin; at least, as an angel I do. But I think there is another definition of good and bad, as opposed to the bad of sinning. I recall Father saying something about it being in terms of right and wrong. There must be a fine line between wrong and bad. I do know that Father said that some men do wrong and don't classify it as sin because it's not bad enough to violate the laws written by man.

Hey, Jim, what's a good child, and what's a bad child?

"Look at Big George, honey. He and Jalil have one thing in common already—they are both good babies. Neither one does any complaining."

Mmm. Not complaining is good, and complaining must be bad. When you need information quickly, angel power has its advantages.

Later in the day I had a crisis, as the staff calls it. They had to go inside my little 'me's' chest and do something.

৪৯ ৪৯ ৪৯

Are not all angels ministering spirits
sent to serve those who will inherit salvation?

DAY 6

So that's what my body looks like! But how did I get out here?

"Got to get him going soon." That's Dr. Miles' voice, although he sounds like an echo off a distant star. He's doing something to my body's chest. Well, I may as well look around while they're doing what they're doing. My chance to see what Jalil looks like, as well as the rest of the place.

He sure doesn't look like me. Must be five times my size. A different color, too. Father had said that His children are different colors. Gosh! Just look at the baby humans! Cute. Not angel cute, but close.

Father once said that babies are as adorable as His angels.

"There, I've got a beat. Susan, ventilate him at sixty percent until his pressure builds."

"Yes, Dr. Miles. Close one, huh?"

"He's a tiger. Got a lot of spunk."

I hear them clearly. No more echo. I'm back inside my body. I believe I was pure angel there for a moment. But, oh, my 'me' hurts. I'm a tiger. Let's see...big Earth animal with orange stripes and big teeth. Another funny Earth comparison, I suppose. I wonder if I'll be here long enough to get used to the way they speak? I really didn't see the comparison. I'm not as big as a tiger. I'm not orange, and I didn't see any stripes when I looked at me. I'm brown. Teeth? I'll check. No—no teeth either.

A lot of spunk?

"Spunk means spirit, George."

Michael?

"Yes, George, it's me. And comparing you to a

tiger means you have a courageous spirit." Michael laughs. "Of course, as an angel, naturally you have a courageous spirit."

Full-fledged angels know a lot. Not as much as Father knows, but still a lot.

Tiger spunk. That's a good one, Michael.

"I'll tell Noah you approve of the way it's defined, George. Now, hush. You need to rest your human body."

Ouch!

"Sorry, George." Susan's voice. "But the shot will ease your pain. Poor darling. I love you."

I love you, too, Sus—

ᨑ ᨑ ᨑ

1 JOHN 3:11

This is the message you
heard from the beginning:
We should love one another.

DAY 7

"Good morning, George."

Great happiness! It's Jim—finger and all.

Morning? Heavens! I must have slept a whole day. I can't be doing that. It's a waste of love to sleep too much. Besides, I can't be sleeping on the job. I have my Father's work to do here.

Good morning, Jim. I love you.

Jim moves his face close to me. "I love you. Your mother and dad love you, too. Don't give up, Big George."

*Give up, Jim? I won't give up. I have to earn my
wings by doing Father's business.*

"How's he doing, Jim?" It's Pat.

Jim smiles. "Well, his grip is still strong, that's for
sure."

Just a little angel muscle, Jim.

Jim laughs lightly. "You know, honey, I just can't
get it out of my head that he's talking to me. It's like a
small child's voice inside my head."

Pat laughs. She has a pretty laugh. I knew an angel
in Heaven who laughed a lot like Pat. "Maybe he is."

"Maybe he has his own angel phone," Jim says.
They both laugh. I laugh, too...but I doubt that
humans are capable of recognizing the laughter of
angels.

When angels laugh, it sounds more like birds
singing.

Angel phone? *Good one, Jim.* I believe Jim has a
concept of our language. Angels have no secrets, so
when we speak, anyone with enough love in their

hearts can hear us. Heart-to-heart talking, Father calls it.

"I think what he's doing, Pat, is talking to my heart."

You're right, Jim, I am.

"I can believe that," Pat says.

You sure can, Pat.

"So, tell me, Big George, what's an angel like you doing in a place like this?" Jim asks with fun in his voice.

"Jim," Pat exclaims with a sharp smile. "Someone's going to hear you and think you're nuts!"

Nuts? Hmm...let me think. Nuts—squirrel food. Sometimes eaten by humans. Doesn't make sense to me, but I'll answer Jim.

Father sent me to remind everybody that we should love one another, Jim.

"You haven't told me yet if he answered you." Pat again. There is playfulness in her face.

"As a matter of fact. he did. But I'm not sure you or anyone will believe what he said."

"Try me."

"Okay. He said, 'Father sent me to remind everybody that we should love one another.'"

Pat smiles. "Well, tell him that Jalil and I said he's doing a good job getting his message across."

Thanks, Pat, I appreciate that.

"He said to tell you he appreciates your comment."

"Jim, would you cut that out and go call the girls."

Jim laughs. "She's always bossing me around, Big George, but I love her. I gotta call Kathy and Beau. But I'll be right back. Don't go away."

I don't have any intentions of going anywhere, Jim, until my work for Father is done.

Jim pulls his finger gently from my grip.

Well, Father, the message is delivered to two of your children. Only about five billion to go.

Gee, at this rate, I'll be down here longer than Methuselah.

ℐℰ ℐℰ ℐℰ

Who endowed the heart with wisdom
or gave understanding to mind?

DAY 8

I like mornings on Earth. Everyone's cheerful.
Jim and Pat always come together in the
mornings, and that allows Jim to spend more time
with me while Pat is with Jalil. I heard Jim talking to
Father this morning. He was asking Father to give us
strength. Maybe Jim doesn't know it, but Father's
strength is in me, and I also draw strength from Jim,
Mom, Dad, Susan, Dr. Miles, Pat—anybody who
comes to watch over me. Father had told me that all
humans draw strength from each other through the
body of love. Love binds men together, He said. Man
is not an island, Father went on to say, as a man of a

powerful mind had written, but man is like the trees of the forests, the insects of Earth's floor, the fish of the sea—where there is one, there is a multitude gathered. The fowl of the air fly together. The fish of the sea swim together. Whoever puts himself away from other men is without Me.

Father said all those things.

You can trust Father. He's wise. He knows everything. But sometimes you have to be wise yourself to figure out some of His answers. To impart his wisdom, Father enjoys talking about faith. Probably because faith troubles man, He said, more than anything else. His favorite faith story was about a human seeking a sign from Father. "It began when he was a young human. Having lost track of Me after his first sin, he sought signs to find his way back to Me. Once he lay in a meadow beneath a tree fresh with spring leaves and said to Me, 'God, if you exist, then have that third leaf from the end, the one on the topmost branch of this tree, fall and land on my nose.'

"Of course I didn't. I only chuckled. As the boy human grew into manhood, he continued to challenge Me to do all things as proof of My existence. He asked Me to give him wings that he might fly. Well, I thought that was rather foolish, as I'd already given him airplanes. He asked Me to turn day into night, and I figured this too was foolish, for each day this happens. He asked Me to let him walk on water, and then he tried to—I suppose to see if I would save him rather than allow him to see Heaven sooner than expected—and he nearly drowned. Throughout his Earth years, he never ceased to seek a sign from Me. Finally, when he was ninety Earth years old, near human death, the Son visited him to prepare him for paradise, and I must say he was astonished to see Jesus. 'Why, Lord,' he implored, 'am I who was of so little faith so blessed?' The Son replied that when a man seeks what he believes to exist—that is the essence of faith."

Susan is telling Jalil's parents it is time for them to leave while his tubes are changed. "Just be about fifteen minutes," Susan says to them, "and you can come back in. You'll have time for a cup of coffee."

I notice I have already mentioned *time* several *times*. I've heard it a lot since I came here. Big humans always seem to speak of time. *Time to eat. Time to go. I don't have enough time. Time's a-wasting.* They just go on and on about time. In Heaven, I'd heard a full-fledged angel ask Father about why humans are given to concerning themselves so much with time.

"Father," the angel had questioned, "even when I was as a human in my apprenticeship, I never understood the clamor over time; it's as if everything was measured—good and bad—in the seconds and minutes of the Earth's turn. I thought that upon my return to Paradise I'd be filled with the knowledge of all things human—yet, time still puzzles me. Why are humans fraught with concern over time?"

Now, when Father wanted to skirt telling you everything He knows, He would speak in riddles, often making us baby angels giggle with delight with His light-humored stories.

I remember Father's face wearing a smile bigger than a planet's rainbow as He responded to the questioning angel: "Beats Me. I made time to vary the beauty of man's life, for without the movement of the stars, suns, moons, all the things of Heaven, there is no change, and, too, as you know, movement is life to them. But I didn't mean for time to be a negative force in their human lives. It probably goes along with the enigma I intended for Creation—everything is perfect, but perfect only for the eye blink that it seems as is. In the next blink, perfection takes on another form of perfection. Perhaps I goofed. Maybe purposefully." Father winked. "All I have created, it seems, is perfect except for man's desire to conquer time. I meant for time to be man's friend, offering an ever-changing aura of the beauty of perfection, like the clouds of Earth constantly changing, and yet, time appears to have become man's nemesis."

That was pretty heavy stuff for a little angel like me.

"But, Father," the angel persisted, "man was created in Your image, and You are perfect."

Father winked again. "Then perhaps I amuse Myself in allowing man choices not allowed My other creations. I am the perfect God of Man, but to some degree I have allowed man to be the imperfect god of himself."

"I understand, Father," the angel said, and he disappeared as vapor before sunlight.

I still don't understand. Perhaps I will when I get back to Heaven. But right now, it's *time* for me to get some shut-eye.

* * *

Voices. Ones I've not heard before. Coming from the area the other side of Jalil. Crying. Big humans. They have the sound of parents.

"Please, Mrs. Russell, please calm down. We can't allow you to upset the other parents." It is Susan's voice.

"Peg, they're doing all they can. Now, you're just going to upset yourself more. Calm down, honey." A man's voice.

"Please don't let my baby die! I don't want my baby to die! God! God! Why are You doing this to me! You answer me, dammit! Answer me!" A mother?

Beep! Beep! Beep! Beep! Beep! Beep!

"Is that my baby? Is that my baby?"

"Doctors Stanton, Williams. Report to ICU. Code Blue. I repeat: Doctors Stanton and Williams. Code Blue."

There's that funny-sounding voice again.

I hear a lot of people rushing about.

"We'd better wait outside, honey." Jim's voice.

"She's fainted!" Susan's. *Who* fainted? What's *fainted*?

"Here comes Dr. Williams." I don't recognize this voice.

"Sedate that mother before she comes around. Get a gurney for her. Anybody coming with Adrenalin?"

So it was the baby's mother who fainted.

"It's on the way, doctor."

"Here, doctor."

Silence. *Come on, say something!*

"Breathe, sweetheart, breathe! Getting anything?"

"Nothing, doctor."

"Instrument tray, Susan."

"Instrument tray, doctor."

"I've got one, doctor. Here. You want gloves?"

"No, no time to glove up. Stand back!"

"Mother's coming around!"

"I said to get her out of here!"

"Forget the gurney. I'll carry her." That's Sammie, male nurse. "Mr. Russell, help me with your wife, please."

"I...I..."

"Helen, help him. He's in shock." Sammie's voice.

They are too late. I feel the angel. The little baby is in Heaven now.

"No good. Lost her. She's gone back to Heaven." There is great sadness in Dr. Williams' voice. I wish I could tell him there is no need to be sad. Heaven is a beautiful place, and no one there knows sadness. Sooner or later, all humans who love Father will go to Heaven. That's what Father said. Our only purpose, as humans, in being here is to return to Father. No need to be sad about it.

"Susan," says Dr. Williams, "take the baby's body to post. I'll be in shortly. Right now I want to see what I can do for the parents."

Besides the little Russell girl, two more of my friends went back to Heaven today. Gosh, I have to stay and tough it out. We special angels have to fight the invitation of the Light. Frankly, though, it is sometimes difficult for me to stay here. I miss the peace and happiness of Heaven, and I miss Father very much. I know He is here with me, but it's not exactly the same as it was in Heaven.

ളⓈ ളⓈ ളⓈ

*"A new command I give you:
Love one another. As I have loved you,
so must you love one another."*

DAY 9

nother beautiful day. (I know days because
Father had told us our human bodies have
built-in clocks.) "Look about you," Father said. "See
the wonders. Is not every day beautiful? Of course it
is. If only My children on Earth could see as My
angels see!" Father is proud of His creation. He calls
it perfect love.

Jim and Pat are here with Jalil. I felt Jim's love on
me, but he hasn't touched me this morning. He
probably thinks I'm asleep...I know what you're
thinking: angels sleep? Yes, we sleep. Let's see...how

do I compare it to Earth to give you understanding?
Got it! Angels sleep as the wind sleeps—awake but
unstirring, in perfect unison with the cosmos.

Back to Jim: Jim never goes a day without
touching me, so I'm sure he'll be over to love me with
his finger as he does with his heart.

Ah. *Love*. I could live on it. Ha! As an angel, I *do*
live *as* it.

"Hi, Big George."

See! Didn't I tell you Jim would be over?

Hi. Jim.

"How's my baby?"

*Make that a two-part question, Jim. As an angel, I
feel heavenly...as usual. As a human baby, I could have a
lot of complaints if I gave in to temptation.*

"Little guy, if the whole world had as much love in
it as you have in you, this ol' world would be a better
place to live. One of these days I'm going to write a
book about you."

Book? Now that would be a great way to spread

Father's message to all His children. Of course, He
already has a Book in publication. Mmm. Well, it is a
very thick Book. Perhaps if His children had a thin
one they could begin with, one that would encourage
them to go back and read Father's Book again...or for
the first time.

Just a little book with a simple message: Love one
another. Anything else is of no matter. As Father
loves us, so must we love one another. As Father said,
"He who hates his brothers and sisters, hates Me."
Father was emphatic when He gave me this message
for His children on Earth. Never before had I heard
Father speak so firmly. Nor with such sadness. Father
wept as He spoke.

"My precious children. Do they not understand
that darkness cannot enter the Light, that hate cannot
live as the Spirit of Love? Hate steals My children
from Me; and I cannot as Love force love upon them.
Love is never overbearing, never consuming. Who I
am prevents Me, though all-powerful I am, from being

other than I am. Fire cannot enter the river, and hate and evil cannot enter love and goodness and be one with them. Only by love can My children return Home to Me. I weep for those I lose."

With his other hand, Jim has touched my face. "Don't you worry, Big George. I hear your heart. I'm in some pretty tough times right now, and I think it's going to get worse before it gets better, but you have my promise on that book, although I may need yours and God's help to write it."

"I see I've got you talking to babies, too."

It's Susan, happy-voiced.

Jim laughs lightly. "I'm not talking to a baby, Susan—I'm talking to an angel."

Of course, Jim doesn't really believe I'm an angel. I know he just thinks of me as an angel. Perhaps if I left my body for a few seconds...maybe flashed the lights, floated a few things...

"George! What did I say about games?"

Just kidding, Father.

"That's better. Now, on Jim—when I decide, Jim will know who you are. But right now you are still as a human baby...so sleep like one."

Sorry, Jim, but I must obey Father.

"You get some sleep, little guy. Pat and I have to go get some lunch. But I'll be back soon. Maybe your parents will show up today or tomorrow."

ℬ ℬ ℬ

1 JOHN 4:2

*This is how you can recognize
the Spirit of God: Every spirit
that acknowledges that Jesus Christ
has come in the flesh is from God.*

DAY 10

I thought I felt Mother and Dad!
*Oh, Mother, your touch is so wonderful.
Please don't cry, Mother.*

"Oh, George, he still hasn't shown any change. I had hopes."

"Now, Sharon, we've been over this time and time again. Maybe it woulda been best if we hadn't come up here. We both know we gonna lose him. Ain't no use putting you through this misery."

"George Hawkins! Don't you say that! Our son needs us, and we gonna come be with him so long as we can find a way up here."

"Now, Sharon, I didn't mean it that way. I just don't like seeing you hurt is all. You know I'm hurt, too. He is one beautiful baby. Impossible not to love and care for him just like he was an older child. I didn't mean no harm in what I said."

"I know, George. He's a child without sin of his own, honey, so I know Jesus will take him to be with Him in Heaven, just as we will one day be in Heaven. We both know Jesus came here as a man to give us Heaven."

"Sure we do, Sharon, and I find peace in that, too."

What a joy to my heart! Mother and Dad are from Father, also. I wonder if they're angels who have been here so many Earth years that they've forgotten how to understand angel language. Gee, maybe we're a family of angels. That would be greater happiness for sure!

Where's my Jim?

"Good morning, Sharon, George. Sure am happy to see you here again."

There's my Jim.

"Good morning, Jim. Good morning, Miss Pat." Dad's voice is a lot like Father's: pure.

"We've been keeping an eye on Big George for you. Incidentally, George, I was thinking...well, if you and Sharon would like to stay here at a motel near the hospital, Pat and I would be pleased to pay for the room and your meals and all. You could ride to and from the hospital each day with us."

"Gosh, Jim, that's awful nice of you and Pat, but we just couldn't accept. I got my job to go to. Might lose it if I missed work for long. Anyhow, we just wouldn't be able to pay you back."

"You don't have to pay us back, Mr. Hawkins," Pat says. "Jim and I would just love to see you and Sharon be able to stay here with Big George."

"Thanks, Miss Pat," Mother says, "but George is right. Wouldn't be right for us to take you all's money like that. You all gonna need your money, too."

"Well, Pat and I are going for a late breakfast. Why don't you and Sharon think it over?"

"We'll do that, Jim. And we sure appreciate you offering."

After Jim and Pat left, Dad says, "Jim's a nice man, and him and his wife wanting to help us stay here with the boy is mighty kind of them, but Sharon, I can see a lot of hurt in that man's eyes. I think we ought to refuse. Those two are going to be out a lot of money. Miss Susan says Jim is losing a lot of money from work. And they don't have any insurance. Because they have money, they'll have to pay their son's bill. Miss Susan said it cost over two thousand dollars a day if the parents have to pay. Sometimes I think we're lucky that we're poor. We'd be in big trouble if we had to pay that kind of money to a hospital." Dad laughs, more like a shy chuckle.

"Maybe it ought to be us offering them help."

"They must be good Christians," Mother says.

Yes, Mother, they are. Jim understands my heart, and I know Father is talking to him about me.

When Pat and Jim returned from breakfast, Dad again refused their offer. No matter. I am so certain of Father's will being in everything that touches my human life, few things bother me...just the pain. Well, the beeper does upset me, too. Earlier this morning one of the beepers signaled a sister's return to Heaven as a spirit.

The rest of my day was spent with Mother and Dad. Only once—when Mother and Dad went to eat—did Jim come over and speak to me. Jim only said three words to me then, but they were the most beautiful words on Earth and in Heaven. "I love you," he said.

ʃaʃaʃa

Do not forget to entertain strangers,
for by so doing some people have entertained
angels without knowing it.

DAY 11

Wish I could understand what it is that Jim and Pat do each morning when they come in. It has something to do with what they call "reading Jalil's charts and x-rays, and checking his gauges." I'd heard Susan explaining these things to them right after Jalil and I first got here. It apparently has to do with when Jalil can go home with them, because Jim keeps saying, "One day we'll come in and there will be significant changes, and we'll be closer to taking him home." Pat cried softly when he said it. But it was happy crying.

"No change in the x-rays, hon," Jim says. "I'm beginning to wonder—Pat! Take your hand off Jalil, and step back!"

Jim's excited! I wonder what about.

"What?" Pat exclaims.

"Move back, darling. I think he reacted to your touch. I want to see if he does again."

Does *what* again?

"Okay, the gauges are kicking again; he's turning color again. Now, touch him again. Let your hand rest on him. Okay...look at the ventilation gauge, and look at Jalil. The gauge has steadied again. See his coloring—it's pink."

"Jim," Pat says, "you don't think..."

"I don't know. Try it again." I'd sure like to know what's going on. "There—gauge is jumping again. Color's turning blue. Touch him again." Blue? When I saw him, he was white with red hair. Father never said a thing about humans being blue or pink. "Back to pink. Steadied again. Susan!"

"Yes, Jim?"

"You want to come over here and see this? Do it again, honey."

"Oh, my gosh!" Susan's happy. I think I'm beginning to understand. "Marie!" That's another nurse here. "Marie, get the staff. Jalil is reacting to his mother's touch. Reacting miraculously!"

They're talking so excitedly and fast I can't keep up with them. I'll catch what I can.

"Doesn't react to me," Susan says. "Jim, have you tried?"

"No, but I will," Jim says. Silence...then, "No, no response to me, either. Pat, do it again. Oh...here are the others. Watch this, Dr. Miles! You see it? Only with Pat's touch. Let them see it again, Pat."

After a moment, Dr. Miles said, "Well, I'll be darned! Jim, I'll never again encourage parents to wait at home. Jalil is definitely improving with Pat's touch. Of course, he's still a sick little boy. Jim, what I said to you about percentages, that I wouldn't give you false hope based on percentages. Well, I've just witnessed an improvement. I believe I can say the percentage of hope, at least, has just risen."

They all have it mixed up a little. Jalil is reacting to love, just as we all do. The touch of love is just stronger than the aura of love. Father told me that; you didn't think He'd send me down here as a messenger of love without making me knowledgeable on the subject of love, did you? I'm—

Beep!

Uh-oh! That's me!

"Big George!"

Beep! Beep! Beep!

...the light beckoning me...

Beep! Beep! Beep! Beep! Beep! Beep!

Jim. I feel Jim's finger. Thank you, Father, I need Jim. Ahhhhh. Pat, too. Thank you, two times, Father.

"You gave us a scare, little fellow."

I didn't mean to, Jim. Pat's fingers are touching me. Wow! Talk about a jolt of love! Wonder if I'm turning pink?

"There's a big heart in that tiny body. Seeing his courage gives me hope, Jim, for Jalil."

"That white bandage is almost as big as he is. You realize this is the second time they've done open heart surgery on him? Susan says all the doctors are mystified. They don't know how he keeps from going back to Heaven."

That's simple. I have to obey Father, do His bidding. *I love all of you very much. The light comes for me, and I want to follow it, but I know I must stay and love. I thank you, Jim, Pat, Susan. Your love—Mother and Dad's—everybody's love is helping me to stay human.*

Oh, if only everyone could hear me! I don't mean just everyone in this place, but everyone in the world. My mission is so important to Father, but I am stuck here in one spot. There must be a way to spread Father's message faster. No telling when Jim will write the book.

"Don't you die, little man."

Die, Jim? He must *know.* There is no death for the children of Father. Jesus saw to that. In the Father, we have eternal life. It is written: Only suns die.

"He's an angel, isn't he?" It's Susan. *Well, yes, Susan, I am. Not a full-fledged angel yet, but I'm working on it.*

"I don't think there's any doubt about that," Jim says.

Pat is crying on me. Her tears feel like Mother's tears. It bothers me that I cause so many tears.

"You know, Susan," says Pat, "it wouldn't surprise me if he is an angel. Jim spends more time with him than I do, but when I'm near him, I feel—does this sound corny?—I feel...well, I feel like I'm in church."

They laugh.

"No, Pat," says Susan, "I don't think it sounds corny at all. Fact is, I feel the same way about him. It's like there's an aura of holiness surrounding him. I feel a glow when I'm around him. Some of the other nurses have said the same about him."

It's not me, of course. They are feeling Father. I know His presence, too. I feel Him constantly. He's been keeping a watch over me.

"People just don't understand what's going on in these centers," Jim says. "I called a man in Florida the other day and told him I'd have to cancel my lecture there because we were staying with Jalil to see him through. Can you believe this: he told me that he could understand if Jalil were older, but that I hardly knew this child. He said he'd sue me if I didn't show for the lecture. It makes you wonder how long you have to live in order to have any rights to life. If that man could be here to look at Big George and Jalil, he'd see that both are 100 percent human. Size has nothing to do with it. I even believe that Big George understands every word we're saying."

Well, not every word, Jim, but most of them.

"Jim," Susan says, "it's not that people can't understand; it's more because it hurts too much to want to understand. A child's suffering is the most difficult thing in life to deal with. To avoid the mental anguish, many people ignore its existence. When I came to work here, the thing that hurt most was seeing the name plaques above the beds. You want to use euphemisms: infant and newborn. But those name plaques force us to see these little humans as real people. Big George will fit into the palm of my hand, but he has every part of his tiny body, and every part is perfectly formed. He sees. He hears. He thinks. Yet, from conception, he is only six-and-a-half months old. We saved a preemie a few months ago who was only two pounds at birth. I believe that in years to come, maybe even in the very near future, we'll be seeing one-pound infants survive."

Saved? We are saved by love.

My body is telling me I'm sleepy...

ജ ജ ജ

It [love] always protects, always trusts,
always hopes, always perseveres.

DAY 12

*J*im and Pat stayed longer yesterday than usual. I'm sure their staying longer had something to do with Pat's love touches. I was happier, not only for Jalil, but for myself, as Jim spent more time with me. I was having one rough day of it, and without Jim I may have been tempted to follow the light.

Pat is aglow this morning.

"Look! He's doing it again!" she exclaims to Dr. Miles.

"Now, Pat, I don't want you two getting your hopes too high. As I said, Jalil is still a sick little boy.

I also want to be frank with you in telling you that your son is on 100 percent oxygen and has been now for twelve days. Prolonged oxygen can do a lot of damage to an infant, even to an adult. I'm not trying to throw cold water on your hope, but I just want you to keep a realistic outlook about his possible recovery."

"Dr. Miles," Jim says, "would you agree that it's been proven that one person can suffer—say, pneumonia of a mild form, and another person can have a severe case of pneumonia, one which might be terminal in the usual course, and the person with the mild case will die, and the person with the severe case will live? And not just with pneumonia, but occurring in other diseases as well, such as cancer?"

"Of course I have, Jim. Now, hold on...I did not say we were going to lose Jalil; I just want you to be prepared."

"Prepared for what—failure? I'm a businessman, Dr. Miles, a writer. I never begin anything prepared for failure, no more than a football player goes into the game prepared to lose gracefully. Pat and I aren't here on a death watch. We're here to see our son pull through."

Wow! A comet couldn't streak through this silence, it's so thick!

It's Dr. Miles who breaks the silence, and I feel the flow of love in his words: "Of course you are, Jim. I believe I've been trying to pass off my defense mechanism on to you."

"You don't need to explain, Dr. Miles. I understand. And I'm sorry for spouting off. Working here must be a strain I'd never understand."

"And perhaps I don't understand what you parents go through. I'm only a doctor here. These are your children. But I want you to know that I love them, too."

"We know you do," Pat says.

Everybody should love everybody.

I thought I'd just toss that in.

"Everybody should love everybody....Good grief! That was strange. I don't even know what possessed me to say it. It just popped into my head!" Well, Pat, I believe you're beginning to understand angel language.

Of course, love in the heart possessed Pat to say that...with a little influence on my part.

They're laughing now, which is what I intended. I like laughter. Laughter lights up my spirit.

"Look at Big George," Jim says. "Looks like he's smiling."

"So he is," says Dr. Miles. "Must be having a good dream.

Well, I've got to make my rounds, Jim, Pat. I'll drop by later."

The rest of the day was almost heavenly. My brothers and sisters mostly slept, and no one returned to Heaven.

ৡ৯ ৡ৯ ৡ৯

*And hope does not disappoint us, because
God has poured out his love into our hearts
by the Holy Spirit, whom he has given us.*

DAY 13

Though my body is in pain all the time, the love here is as the doves of Heaven flickering about in the heart of Father. It soothes the human me. The Holy Spirit in me builds a fire of strength for me to draw on, and I'm knowledgeable that the Holy Spirit is not only in the hearts of angels, but in the hearts of all humans who love and adore Father, accepting His will.

Father said some humans do not understand the Holy Spirit, that it puzzles them to think of Him as a Trinity. But it was simple, really, when He explained it for my benefit.

Father is One who is Three. (Pretty great power, huh, making three out of one?) He said He's so busy all the time, He kind of clones Himself to get things done. Father is Father; the Son and the Holy Spirit are of Father, same as your mind is of you and so is your heart of you. The Son is in charge of forgiving. The Holy Spirit takes charge of our hearts. And Father takes charge—period. That's the explanation He gave me. I'm sure there are other explanations for people not as little as I am.

Father, however, stated that understanding Love, which is Father, isn't the big deal. It's just the end result that counts. He says we can see Him as a bed of roses or as the morning sun, so long as the roses or the sun cleanses our hearts of evil and has us love all things as we are loved. Father just doesn't want us to argue about understanding. I recall exactly what He said: "Lucifer loves argument. His favorite tactic is to create religious dissent, or to start wars, or as fuel for charlatans. Love Me. Love one another. Do good. Keep My commands. I know your hearts. It is not the manner of your understanding so much as it is your love for Me and your fellow man."

Beep! Beep! Beep! Beep! Beep! Beep!

Not me. Not Jalil. Three have already returned to Heaven today. I never knew it before I came here, but there must be a lot of little spirits in Heaven.

Susan told me today that Mother and Dad phoned to ask about me. I know my parents are not able to be here with me all the time, although I wish they could be. I need all the love touches I can get. Father, a guardian angel told me, wants parents to be with their children, but the angel went on to say that my parents' not being here was Father's way of getting Jim to know me better. Whatever the reason, I accept Father's will.

Jim often tells me how much he loves me. Of course, I can angel-feel how much he does, as well as human-feel his love, but it's always great to hear one is loved. I like the sound of the word.

Despite missing Heaven, and Mother and Dad not being with me all the time, I'm a happy angel. Perhaps I can be called a Twinity. Ha ha! I just thought that was funny. Twins were brought in this morning, weighing three pounds each, and everybody is excited. Twin girls. They're fine, I heard. In a big incubator. Going to be here a long time as humans.

Sometimes I feel a great void, and in those times I feel the human side of me stronger than usual, as though that part of me yearns to remain on Earth as long as possible. The angel in me, however, is aware.

Blessed are those whose strength is in you,
who have set their hearts on pilgrimage.

DAY 14

"Come on, George, let's have a beat...thatta boy! You can do it."

My little chest feels like a comet hit me.

"How does he do it?"

"I don't know. A healthy adult couldn't withstand what this little guy's been through. I really thought he'd return to Heaven on this one. Just tack him shut; we may have to go in again."

"It does stagger the imagination, doesn't it? He may have set a record for surviving heart failure. Thank God he's got the strength he has."

My strength is in Father. My heart is set on becoming a full-fledged angel, on pleasing Father. Do not brag on me. Revere Father. He alone is great. Neither man nor angels are to be revered. No, Father did not need to tell me that. To know Father, is to *know*.

"I saw Jalil's parents on the way in. How long now?"

"Two weeks—all day and most of the night. They're strong, particularly the mother. She either hides it well, or she's the stronger of the two. Pat's her name. The man is Jim. He appears on the verge of tears most of the time. But it's beginning to show more on both of them."

"I heard about their son responding well to his mother's touch. What's the prognosis?"

"If you'd asked a week ago, I'd have told you zero. Right now, I don't know. He's spunky. Good weight. Heart's good. We've been working with Emory Hospital in Atlanta to come up with a drug to fight his adult pneumonia virus. Miles is worried about the prolonged oxygen. If we don't get him to do some of his breathing soon, the oxygen could have serious aftereffects. Oh, on the mother's touch bit—others have been checking to see if it's made a difference in their children, and I'm happy to say, it has. We've never kept records on it, but I wouldn't be surprised that the survival rate would come up higher if we had a means of helping all the parents remain with their children. Got to be costing Jim and Pat a fortune to remain here. They're from Texas."

I have no idea who these voices belong to, but I find them interesting.

Beep! Beep! Beep! Beep! Beep! Beep!

It's not me.

"Janie Doe." Susan's voice. "Our mystery girl. She's stopped trying to breathe again."

"Mystery girl?" Their voices are moving away from me.

"Yes. A little chest pressure usually starts her up. There, thatta girl. Yes, mystery girl. Mystery who her parents are. Police brought her in three days ago after she was found abandoned at the bus station. She was only a few hours old."

"She going to be okay?"

"We think so. She's a little stubborn about breathing. I don't know, maybe she doesn't want to breathe, doesn't want to live without her mother. Perhaps she wants to return to Heaven. I think she just misses her mother. Miles says she's almost full term. Just breaks my heart when something like this happens, both for the child and the mother. You want to hate the desperate little thing who left this child, but I guess somewhere in life love left her, too."

Love is Father, Susan. It never leaves us, not if we stay strong in Father. I will talk to Father about His child who is without its mother.

"You know, Marie," says Susan, "I have a hunch this is one mother who's going to come forward."

The rest of the day, each time I came out of sleep, Jim was at my side. Through conversations, I learned later that three of my friends returned to heaven today. I must have been asleep when they left.

*When he [Jesus] saw the crowds, he had
compassion on them; they were harassed and
helpless, like sheep without a shepherd.*

DAY 15

The days between seeing Mother and Dad are difficult for me, and although I know my time as a human is near to a close, the human emotion of sadness is not for myself, as Father prepared me, but for my parents, for Jim, Pat, Susan. It is my wish for them to know that Heaven brings us all together in full knowledge of the humans we were. The only thing we have no memory of, Father says, is death. "You cannot remember that which does not happen," Father said. But my immediate problem is *how?* How do I impart to Mother and Dad, Jim and Pat, and

Susan, the knowledge that we will know each other in Heaven? Perhaps I can find out in prayer.

Father, this is Big George. I have a prob—

"I know. It is written in My Book that families and friends will be brought together in Heaven."

What if they haven't read that part?

"If they read, they should have. But I'm aware your parents cannot read or write, George, so I will tell them for you. Faith will give them knowledge; love will teach them the truth."

Thank you, Father, I knew I could count on You. That takes a load off my mind. Er... Father, one more thing before You turn Your attention to other matters.

"I know what it is, child," Father says patiently. "It is about your parents not being taught to read or write."

Exactly, Father. Don't all humans read and write?

"They should be taught, but many are not. Some of mankind keep them from the knowledge of reading and writing, hoping that it will leave them ignorant, that man who seeks riches may use their ignorance for his personal gain. At least, man *thinks* this is the reason for his suppression of other men's knowledge. The true reason is that some men fear the knowledge of others. When man understands that My Son wrote not with a pen but through the hearts of men, he'll be aware all knowledge is of the heart and not of the mind. Reading and writing are not essential to good wisdom."

Do my parents have good wisdom, Father?

Father smiles. "They are My children, and I chose them to be your Earth parents. I gave them wisdom of understanding and love. I gave wisdom to all my creations, George. Does the sparrow build its nest safe from the storm? Of course it does, and it is one of the lesser of My creations; man is My highest creation."

What is the greatest wisdom, Father?

"To obey compassion. Compassion will soothe the angry beast, bring solace to the sick of heart, and defeat evil. He who allows compassion to rule his actions allows Me to rule his heart."

Isn't compassion love, Father?

"Compassion is the true Spirit of Love. It is the wood that feeds the fire of the heart."

Then I have nothing to be concerned about?

"Wrong. You have much to be concerned about, George." Father smiled. "You still have My bidding to do."

Whew! It's getting tougher every day being an angel!

Jim. Where are you, Jim? I need a finger to lean on.

🙵 🙵 🙵

*Those who obey his commands live in him
and he in them. And this is how we know
that he lives in us: We know it by the Spirit he gave us.*

DAY 16

Susan just remarked that this has been an uneventful day. She sounded happy about it, however. Susan's silly sometimes. Father told us there is no such thing as uneventful. One day to Him, Father said, is a thousand Earth days. So much to do in His limitless Kingdom! It staggers the human mind, He went on to say, how He handles it all. He chuckled and explained: "They find it difficult to understand the all-present, all-knowing mind, thinking of Me within the same limits they impose on creation. I often think that in their 'scientific' search for truth, for the answer to creation, their true search is not for the imaginary wall of Heaven, but for the concreteness of My existence, My power. Of course, I sometimes wonder that perhaps they seek to disprove Me. Humans have their sayings: 'If the truth were known...' and 'My theory of space is...' Funny thing is, the truth is known. Theory is a pet laugh of Mine, particularly when pertaining to space." Father's laugh shook Baby Heaven. "Doesn't take much intelligence to figure that one out—space is limitless. I am also perturbed that they 'interpret' Me. This I resent. It's like telling Me I don't know how to present My thoughts clearly. Oh, to interpret Me for goodness in any form is quite all right, but to interpret Me for harm, to avoid keeping My commands, is a grave sin. For example, I said, 'You shall not kill.' Surely, man has a right to protect himself from injury, and this, if righteous, modifies My commandment. But man kills to keep property; man kills to defend *his* religion.

Man comes up with a lot of false justification for killing. Again, I say, 'You shall not kill.'"

One little angel said seriously, "Father, perhaps you should write the commandments again for Your children."

Father chuckled. "Yes...and I should be sure there are large periods at the end of each one of them."

Father then spoke to a guardian angel: "Child, what is the proof of My all-present, all-knowing Self?"

"Faith, Father."

"And?" Father prodded.

"You *are*."

"Exactly. Well spoken, child. I *am*. As one on Earth might say, 'I *am*...like it or lump it.'"

A baby angel asked Father, "What about when You rested, Father? Were You unwatching then? It is written that You rested."

Father smiled. "I rest as a mother with a newborn child rests—with one eye open."

It was at this point that Father told of uneventfulness.

"The cosmos is never without events of greatness. I can and do take nothingness and turn it into event-fulness. A part of My greatness is this. For man, the beauty of life is always eventful. But to find event, one must seek. In My case, however, My days are eventful without much seeking on My Part. Prayers of man keep Me busy. Often, man's prayers are repeated again and again, although I answered them the first time I was asked. Let me tell you about one of My favorites.

"There was this man, a good man whose goodness I appreciated, who lived to the west of a mountain, a high mountain that blotted out the sun until almost noon, Earth time. Well, he prayed that I might help him move the mountain so that his home could feel the morning sun. Now, all-knowing that I am, I really thought it would be best if he just moved out of the mountain's shadow, but he insisted I help him move the mountain. To reward his love for Me,

I answered his prayer. Time passed. The mountain
remained. And the man importuned Me many times
to move the mountain. Finally, I told him that I'd
answered his prayer long before, that I had sent
him a—"

"A shovel!" squealed a baby angel with delight.

Father smiled and winked. "Close, child. But, as
I told you, this was a very good man. I sent him a
bulldozer. That's a machine that moves mountains
much easier and faster than a shovel. I'd given man
the knowledge to move mountains, but often they
pester Me to do it for them."

"Are You saying, Father," a baby angel asked,
"that man's prayers are often requests for something
he already has?"

"Yes."

"What should man pray for, Father?"

"To see with his inner eye. The Spirit is in man;
I am man's inner eye. To see as I see, man must be in
constant communication—prayer—with Me."

"I see, Father," said the same baby angel. "Prayer to accept Your will. But I am a baby angel, Father. How do I know these things that man seems not to know?"

"Because you are of pure Spirit, child. You are Spirit without the flesh of man."

"Are there any in the flesh of mankind who see with Your inner eye, Father?"

"There are many. Other men see them as mere humans, but they are My angels in disguise."

"Are these the poor, Father?"

"The poor are My Son in disguise."

"Do Your angels on Earth see Your wonders with constant eye?"

"When one sees man watch the sunset, or smiles in amazement at the face of a child, or sits listening to the birds singing...one is seeing a child of mine who has discovered that every moment of life is indeed eventful."

I could just go on and on telling you of the wonders of Father! Hey! Here are Jim and Pat. Not that I was bored. I was just lying here enjoying the wonder of a light bulb. Oh, but I love talking about the things I learned from Father.

Also, Susan's not silly, not really. Just an expression of mine. Also an expression of hers, I'm sure. You and I both know what she meant about this being an uneventful day.

"Hi, Big George," Jim says. "How's God's little angel?"

Oh, just lying here being thankful for the eventfulness of Creation, Jim.

Jim smiles heavily on me. "In my opinion, you are one of the biggest events in Creation."

*Therefore, whoever humbles himself like
this child is the greatest in the kingdom of heaven.*

DAY 17

*I*s it Mother I feel?

"There, darling, Mama's here. Your Daddy's here, too. We love you."

I love you too, Mom, Dad.

"We're going to lose you, George. We know we're gonna lose you. The Lord is a very good Lord, but we know. We accept His will."

You are blessed, Mother.

Father, may I tell Mom and Dad I'm an angel? It is not for my pride, but for their hearts, Father.

"It is your choice, My child."

My choice? I must think this over. They say that I
have given strength to other parents...not as an angel,
for they know me not for sure as an angel, but as a
human.

Father disguises His angels so that faith remains
based in the eye of the heart rather than the eye of
the mind. If my secret became known, faith in love
would be based on the angel side of me, rather than
the human side. Father, I believe, seeks for man to
find the strength of love in his fellow man as well as
in Him. No, I must not reveal myself as an angel. I
feel Father's smile on me. I have made the right choice.

"Sharon, we'll have another baby."

"George, I know we will. But I can't get it out of
my mind that something's special about our boy. All
those nice things people say about him. How brave he
is. Miss Susan says she thinks he's an angel. And that
Mr. Jim and his wife. I ain't ever met folks like them.
They seem to love George as much as we do. Maybe
he is an angel, honey. Maybe God sent us an angel to

help bring folks together, help us all love each other. You think that might be so, George?"

"Now, Sharon, you just imagining things. We just poor folks from the country. The Lord's got better folks than us to send down angels to."

"Well, George Hawkins, Joseph and Mary were poor folks, too!"

Silence.

Mother's voice was firm but loving, like when a guardian angel speaks.

"Okay, Sharon, maybe there is some angel in him. One thing's for certain, he sure looks like one."

Father, you sneak! You told them!

Mother kisses me. Then Dad.

It was the most beautiful day of my life. I will remember it eternally.

Then Jesus said to her,
"Your sins are forgiven."

DAY *18*

Sometime after Mother and Dad left last night, a guardian angel came to visit me. I was happy to see him. It had been difficult for me to have my parents leave, knowing for them it will be a long time before they see me again. For me, though, I believe the time will be no more than the blink of Father's eyes before I am with them forever. Knowing this, I did not complain to the guardian angel, whose name was Mark, because I know that special angels should not complain. It is not heavenly, as I said, to complain. Anyway, Mark just smiled in on me. Checking on me, he said.

Jim and Pat have gone to lunch. My food, as Jesus said, is to do the will of Him who sent me and to finish His work.

Things have been quiet except for babies crying in the nursery. I worry about these things, like crying and food, even though I've been assured that just because I've never tasted food and never cried doesn't mean that I haven't fully experienced human life. I mean, I wouldn't want to miss out on anything that might mess up my qualifying as a full-fledged angel.

I hear the door. Perhaps it's Jim and Pat returning from lunch.

"Right over here, hon." No, it's Susan with someone. Whoever Susan is with is crying. Sounds like the sobbing of a young female.

"Janie," Susan says, "this is your mother...but I suppose I don't need to tell you that, do I? Go ahead, Linda, you can pick your daughter up."

Thank you, Father, You made my day.

"I...I didn't want to leave you... What did you call my baby?"

"I called her Janie. That's what we call lost babies. But you can name her whatever you like. She's your little girl, you know."

"I think Janie is pretty. Are they going to let me keep her?"

"Well," says Susan, "if they had other ideas, I don't believe the police would have brought you here. It took a lot of love to come back for her knowing you could have gone to jail. Yes, I'm sure you're going to get to keep her."

"I won't ever leave her again, ma'am. I just hope that God will forgive me for leaving her in the first place."

What was her name? Oh yes—*Linda, Father always forgives those who hope for His forgiveness. Father loves everybody. He Himself said He is incapable of not forgiving, of not loving.*

He explained this in Baby Heaven: "If I am Love, how can I hate? If I am Compassion, how can I not forgive? The Son of Man stated clearly and absolutely Who I am: I am the God of Love. I love My enemies. I show compassion to those who would destroy Me. I do good unto those who would hate Me. As a good parent sets example, I set example for My children. Love finds no solace in hate or revenge. My tears are the solace for My children's injuries. The fallen angels exist not of their power but of My compassion, as a wicked child uses his parents' love to continue his wrongdoing, taking advantage of that which I am: Love. Love is helpless to bring injury to another. Love always forgives."

Linda has Father's love and forgiveness. She will, I know, be a good mother to her child, Janie.

Jim and Pat have just returned. They are happy, too, about this mother and child. As soon as they've finished sharing their joy, perhaps Jim will give me a day's fingerholding.

ৡৡ ৡৡ ৡৡ

DAY 19

I'm beeping more today. The light comes and goes, and a guardian angel keeps peeping in on me. Sometimes I can just see his face in the light. Other times I feel the fullness of him as he comes to escort one of my brothers or sisters to Heaven. It seems that the guardian angel is familiar to me from Baby Heaven, as though I know him well, but the connection is vague.

"Jim, I don't know how much more of this I can take." It's Pat. Poor darling. "That little girl this morning...I...can't bear to see another one return to Heaven, Jim."

"You want to take the girls and go home, let me stay here with Jalil?"

"No, no, of course not. I just don't understand is all. How can God allow this to happen, I mean?"

"Hon, I don't believe it's God's doings. Like with Jalil—had I left you and the girls home, none of this would have happened. No, I had to insist you come along on this trip. It's my fault Jalil's here. Not yours. Not God's. Mine."

"Now, Jim, don't go blaming yourself again. It was my choice to come along. Anyway, Dr. Stevens did the sonogram and approved the trip for me."

I wish they could hear me as a human; I'd interject something at this point. I believe Father planned for Jim and Pat and Jalil to be here with me. I recall what Father said about faults. First, He worries about faults of His children, people blaming themselves, true or otherwise. Sometimes, He said, a fault is true when something happens to a child. I'd heard Him tell a full-fledged angel that mothers and fathers have a lot of responsibility toward their little ones, and this responsibility begins at conception. The body is Father's temple on Earth, and to do bad things to His temple upsets Him. Not only because it endangers little ones inside the mother, but as it also injures the mother, whom Father loves. He went on to say that when a human does bad to the body, the result of that badness is not His fault or anyone's other than the spirit occupying the body.

"I gave them choice," Father said. "If one wishes to climb a dangerous mountain for no reason other than to climb it, then falls and suffers bodily death, that's his choice, not Mine. Same thing applies if one is walking and doesn't watch where he's going and gets hit by a truck. Again, not My doing—his." Father went on to say further that we should not tempt Him. He explained that this meant we should not deliberately get ourselves into trouble and expect Him to extract us from our own doing.

"But You often do extract them, Father," a baby angel said.

And Father replied sadly, "I know...but sometimes I must give them miracles to feed their faith."

Anyway, I have a strong feeling that Jalil's being here is not Jim's or Pat's fault. As I have heard Jim and Pat talk with the staff and to each other, a lot of strange things have happened. First, Jim was born at this hospital. Then Jalil's name. In a language from the other side of Earth, besides "great friend," his name also translates to "Jesus." The ambulance bringing Jalil here was named "Angel One." My parents have no money. Jim and Pat have money, I've heard. This is what they call a charity hospital for those who have no money. Why is Jalil here if Jim and Pat have money? According to the staff, Jalil and I were to return to Heaven immediately, yet both of us are still here nineteen Earth days later—

Beep!

"Susan! Big George again!"

It's okay, Jim—false alarm.

Now, where were we? Oh, yes—faults. Anyway, I believe that Jalil and Jim and Pat have something to do with the message that Father has me delivering. Like Jalil's name—a reminder that Jesus was once in the form of man. No, I'm sure Jalil is not another Jesus. There is only one Jesus. Father knows how dramatic humans are, so Jalil and Angel One and other "coincidences" were probably just arranged by Father to set the scene for my message.

Be-Beep!

Hush! I'm not going to return to Heaven until Father is ready, so you can *Beep! Beep!* all you want to, and it's not going to do any good. I don't mean to lose my human temper, but when the beeper keeps going off, Jim touches me less. Perhaps he's afraid he'll hurt me.

Well, I could be wrong—I feel Jim's finger nudging my hand.

ℰ ℰ ℰ

Anything you ask in my name,
I will do for you.

DAY 20

"Hello, George."

What are you doing here, Jesus?

"I've come to prepare you for your return to Paradise. Father is well pleased with you."

But I have done nothing, Jesus. I am so little. I have failed to do Father's bidding, though I tried with all my human heart and angel spirit.

"You have done *nothing*, George? You have placed the strength of love in the hearts of men and women. That is not nothing...that is everything."

But so few hearts, Jesus. So few hearts.

"From a seed grows a forest, child."

Jalil...Jesus, may I ask You for something?

"Anything you ask me in my name, I will do for you. Tell me what it is you wish, child."

Allow Jalil to remain here with his Earth parents. Make him well.

Jesus smiles. "Jalil will know many Earth years, George. He is to remain as a part of Father's plan. Through Jalil and you, the strength of love will grow in Jim. But it will take many Earth years for Jim to understand that Father had His plan for Jalil, him, and you, George. When your brother returns to escort you to be in Paradise with me, Jim will falsely think he did not love you enough."

What? Not Jim! Jim loved me enough, Jesus. This cannot be!

"It must be, child."

Why, Jesus, why?

"It is complex for the human side of you, George, and probably will be for all humans, but I will try to give you understanding. In Heaven's language, let's say that it is easy to love when everything is golden, as it is in Heaven. But great love on Earth requires unyielding love for one another, unyielding love for Father, not only when life is golden, but when life's ordeals shadow one's life."

You mean that Father is testing Jim?

Jesus touches my face, smiles reassuringly.

"No, little one. Father is merely allowing Jim to discover for himself that he not only loved you enough, but loved you more than he did himself. This is the greatest love, child: to love one another without any hint of selfishness. What Jim feared will never come to pass."

But will Jim suffer, Jesus, until he realizes this?

Jesus bends to kiss me.

"Love endures, child. Love endures."

I love you, Jesus.

"I know, George, I know. Now, I must return to Father."

Must you leave, Jesus?

"Ah, little one, have you truly grasped the message? Fear not, for I am always with you."

My little 'me' blushes. Now I know what Jesus has been explaining to me, although I missed the main point: There is never anything to fear—not for Jim, not for me, not for you, because Jesus is always with us. Jim's faith is to be rewarded—Jim *knows.*

I understand now, Jesus.

"Good. I will see you shortly in paradise....Oh, and I almost forgot what I came here to tell you: Father sends you a message."

Yes, Jesus?

"Leave behind the notion of sticking others with sharp objects." Jesus winks. I giggle. He becomes Light.

Weakened in body, but not in Spirit, my little 'me' slept the rest of the day.

ၜခ ၜခ ၜခ

The
Return

DAY 21

Jesus is a Man of His Word.

Jim and Pat should be here soon to share in the good news. Are they going to be happy! There was a lot of happiness this morning when Susan came in. Jalil, of course, is doing a lot of his own breathing for the first time. The staff is excited. Nothing like a miracle to stir things up, to excite humans. Oh, Jim and Pat are here now.

"Good morning, Susan," says Jim. "You look as if you just drank a bottle of sunshine. Any change in our son?"

Jim has asked that question twenty times now. I can feel the beauty of Susan's smile. "I've a reason to be happy. But see for yourselves. Jalil took a miraculous turn last night. Darlene and the staff doctors said he just kept getting better and better as the night progressed. They're calling it spontaneous remission. Dr. Miles says he's never seen anything like it. In a matter of hours, Jalil was weaned down to 25 percent oxygen and ventilation. Usually takes a day after a child begins to come down before it can be reduced that much. No other word for it—a miracle. Your son's going to be fine now."

Pat is crying. The sound of her crying is changed somehow, different from all the times I've heard her cry before. Like doves cooing to Father in happiness.

Something like that. Difficult for me to describe in Earth language. It is more of a heavenly sound.

"Look at those blue eyes, darling," Jim says. "I think he's looking for you. How's Big George, Susan?"

I feel the darkness of human sorrow. "He...he had a rough night. Darlene says she doesn't know how he made the night. As Jalil got better, Big George took a turn toward the worse. Dr. Miles is calling his parents this morning to ask them to come in. We don't expect him to make it more than a few hours at most."

I feel Michael approaching; my heavenly senses are much stronger in me. I will see my Earth parents in Heaven later.

"No chance at all, Susan?" Jim asks.

"Jim, who can say? None of us thought Jalil would survive. He's the first infant that seriously ill to survive in this center. It leaves us with hope for any child. Love has produced a miracle."

Father is love, Susan.

"Come into the light, my little brother." Michael is here.

Before my human eyes close, I see Pat and Susan hugging each other. What I will miss most about human life will be the hugs my little 'me' could never have.

Jim says, "I think I'll spend a little time with him. Aowh!"

"What's wrong, Jim?" Pat says.

"I...don't know. I started toward Big George and I got—well, it felt like I got shocked, like a spark of static electricity. More tickled than hurt. Funny."

I smile, but do not speak to tell Jim that he was just kissed by an angel.

Beep!

"Let go, brother," Michael says.

Beep! Beep!

"Oh! God! No!"

My Jim...My Jim.

Beep! Beep! Beep! Beep! Beep! Beep!

My human suffering is gone. The Light is my life, my greater happiness, the salvation of me and all souls, and I am of the Spirit. Michael's hand takes mine.

"Am I a full-fledged angel now, my brother?"

Michael smiles and lights Earth's morning clouds with golden rays, then releases my hand, but does not speak. No matter. Entering the golden skies of Heaven, Father's luminance glittering my wings, I am fully aware of who I am.

REVELATION 1:8

I am the ALPHA and the
OMEGA says the Lord God.

❦ ❦ ❦